# Classic
# Cocktails

## Caroline Westmore

Photography by Peter Wakeman

Design by Sam Grimmer

MUD PUDDLE BOOKS, INC.
New York, New York

# acknowledgments

The author would like to thank the following people and organisations for their help in preparing this book: My assistant Jane and Peter the photographer for their hard work, affection and incredible sense of fun. Our mothers, Claire, Margi and Gwenda, to Linda and Kirsty at Kraft and Tami at McCormick for allowing me to raid their kitchen cupboards. Everyone at Albert Park Fruit Palace, especially Jason and Joe; Australian Hospitality Dinnerware for their beautiful glasses and plates; and Breville for their shiny new appliances. The adorable Sam for making the book so funky; Brigid for crossing my t's and dotting my i's so often and with good humour; Louise for taking the bull by the horns; and Steve and Tracey for conceiving the project.

Published by
Mud Puddle Books, Inc.
54 W. 21st Street
Suite 601
New York, New York 10010

info@mudpuddlebooks.com

© 2001 Hinkler Books Pty Ltd
17-23 Redwood Drive
Dingley VIC 3172 Australia)
www.hinklerbooks.com

Art Director: Sam Grimmer

All rights reserved. Without limiting the rights under copyright above, no part of this publication may be reproduced, stored in or introduced into a retrieval system, or transmitted in any form or by any means (electronic, mechanical, photocopying, recording or otherwise), without the prior written permission of the publisher.

ISBN 1-59412-056-0

Printed in China.

# Introduction

This cocktail book is not for the purist! Apart from traditional cocktails, it contains contemporary and easy-to-mix drinks that are delicious and impressive but only require moderate mixing skills and a home bar stocked with a few essentials.

## equipment

Mixing a good cocktail is indeed an art and it is important to have the right tools. The most important piece of equipment is a jigger. This is usually available as a 30 ml (1 fl oz) and 15 ml (½ fl oz) measure. Although some people like to pour cocktails without using the measure, it is probably not a good idea unless you are a professional barman. Most cocktails are delicate balances of flavours and this subtlety can be ruined by trying to give a drink that generous 'extra dash'.

It is also important to have a good quality cocktail shaker with a glass or metal mixing attachment. Make sure the fit is snug without being tight. The cocktail shaker will also need to be accompanied by a metal strainer, as cocktails such as the Martini and Cosmopolitan require a smooth consistency. The strainer fits wire side down over the shaker and is held in place with the index figure of the pouring hand so that the drink is strained as it is poured.

The last piece of necessary equipment is a good hand juicer or citrus reamer. Fresh juice from fruits such as lemons, limes and oranges are an integral part of many cocktails.

Other useful, although not essential equipment, includes a bar spoon (used to layer shooters, mix ingredients and crush fresh herbs), a muddler (which looks like the stick from a mortar and pestle and is used to muddle or crush herbs), a good bar blender and an ice pick.

The cocktails in this book only require the essential equipment listed above. Substitutes for the rest of the equipment can usually be found in the kitchen drawer.

## glassware

There are some glasses that are essential. Your kitchen cupboard may hold a myriad of glasses, some matching, some not, but a cocktail party requires a little style. The most useful glass to have is, of course, a cocktail glass. This elegant little glass is referred to as a Martini glass in the recipes but is used for countless other drinks such as the Gimplet and the Maiden's Prayer (or Between the Sheets depending upon the number you've had!). You will also need a short tumbler and a long glass for the Old Fashioned and High Flyer drinkers.

Naturally you can buy all sorts of different glasses. A beautiful tulip glass, an elegant champagne flute or a large Margarita glass never goes astray so look for opportunities to add to your collection.

# mixing

The first rule when making cocktails is that the drink is properly chilled. A warm Planter's Punch or a less than frosty Cosmopolitan can deflate the spirits in more ways than one! It is a good idea to freeze the alcohol – it will not solidify in your freezer. Secondly, clean and polish all your glasses (make sure that there is no moisture left in them), then place them in the freezer. This gives the glasses a perfect frost and helps keep the cocktail at the right temperature. Thirdly, use plenty of good, cold ice. This might sound crazy, but using ice that is already melting will dilute the drinks.

Shake, muddle, mix or flash blend the cocktail as required, then strain or pour into the frosted glasses. If pouring several drinks, half-fill each glass, then pass over the glasses a second time to top up. This ensures that each drink is well-blended and makes it easier for you to gauge the levels in each glass.

Always wash and chill your cocktail shaker between each drink, as a warm shaker or leftover taste could create a less than pleasant blend.

# garnishing

Garnishes are an indispensable part of cocktail making. In some cases it makes the drink. After all, a Gibson is a Martini with a cocktail onion rather than a stuffed olive. Remember that simplicity is often the ultimate style guide. More than two garnishes is a sure sign of greed. Overloading a delicious drink with a fruit salad and countless umbrellas is not the way to impress!

# the bar

It would be very easy to spend up big when you stock your bar. It is a better idea to start small and add to your bar with experience. There are, however, some essentials that you should have and which you can use to make quite a variety of drinks.

### gin
The delicious result of the Juniper berry, this spirit is essential for a number of cocktails, including possibly the most famous cocktail of them all – the Martini.

### vodka
Vodka is meant to be almost flavourless but a good quality vodka improves the blend of a drink. The most popular brands are Stolichnaya, Absolut and Smirnoff. Flavoured vodka is also available and provides variety.

**rum**  Rum can be very refreshing in punches and long drinks. The most useful kinds are probably white and golden rum, although a dark rum may be added to a drink for another depth of flavour.

Other drinks that you can gradually add to your bar include whisky, brandy, aniseed-based drinks such as Pernod and tequila, the triple sec family (Cointreau, blue and white curaçao) and flavoured schnapps. To make sugar syrup combine one cup of sugar with one cup of hot water. Stir to dissolve then chill.

For those of you who feel the need to measure, the following may be useful!

a whiff = 1 teaspoon,
a dash = 2 teaspoons,
a splash = 3 teaspoons

| CONVERSION INDEX | 1 teaspoon = 5 ml | |
| --- | --- | --- |
| Remember to | 1 cup (250 ml) | |
| carefully follow either | | |
| metric or imperial | METRIC | IMPERIAL |
| weights and | 30 ml | 1 fl oz |
| measures. Never use | 250 ml | 8 fl oz |
| a combination of | 30 g | 1 oz |
| both, as they are not | 250 g | 8 oz |
| exact equivalents. | 500 g | 16 oz (1 lb) |

# Andy's Ivory

**1 ripe banana**
**60 ml (2 fl oz) banana liqueur**
**30 ml (1 fl oz) Kahlua**
**30 ml (1 fl oz) Bailey's Irish Cream**
**2 cups crushed ice**

Peel the banana. Blend all the ingredients
in a blender until smooth. Pour into two
long or tulip glasses and serve chilled.

Serves two

andy'

savory

black<sub>r</sub>

# ussian

## Black Russian

**60 ml (2 fl oz) vodka**
**30 ml (1 fl oz) Kahlua**
**1 cup crushed ice**
**ice cubes**
**maraschino cherry**

Place the vodka, Kahlua and crushed ice in a
cocktail shaker. Shake, then strain into a
tumbler filled with ice cubes. Garnish with a
maraschino cherry.

Serves one

*You can make a White Russian by adding 30
ml (1 fl oz) of single cream over the top of
the drink, using the back of a spoon.*

# Black Velvet

**45 ml (1½ fl oz) chilled Guinness**
**45 ml (1½ fl oz) white sparkling**
**wine or Champagne**

Half-fill a frosted champagne flute with
Guinness, then top up with the sparkling
wine of your choice.

*Make sure you leave the Guinness to*
*settle in the glass before slowly*
*adding the sparkling wine.*

Serves one

ck velvet

bloody m

# Bloody Mary

**60 ml (2 fl oz) vodka**
**120 ml (4 fl oz) tomato juice**
**15 ml (¹/₂ fl oz) lemon juice**
**1 cup ice cubes**
**pinch of salt and pepper**
**2 dashes of Worcestershire sauce**
**2 dashes of Tabasco sauce**

Pour the vodka, tomato and lemon juice into
a cocktail shaker over the ice cubes and
shake sharply. Pour into a long glass and
then season with the salt and pepper and
the sauces. Serve with a celery stalk.

Serves one

ary

# Cosmopolitan

**30 ml (1 fl oz) vodka**
**30 ml (1 fl oz) Cointreau**
**15 ml (¹/₂ fl oz) lime juice**
**1 splash cranberry juice**
**1 cup ice cubes**
**4 cranberries (optional)**

Pour the vodka, Cointreau and juices into a cocktail shaker over the ice cubes. Shake, then strain into a frosted glass.

Garnish with cranberries if desired.

Serves one

# cosmo

politan

dai

# quiri

## Daiquiri

**45 ml (1½ fl oz) golden rum**
**30 ml (1 fl oz) lime juice**
**15 ml (½ fl oz) sugar syrup**
**1 cup of ice cubes**

Shake all the ingredients in a cocktail shaker. Strain into a frosted Martini glass.

For an icy Daiquiri, flash blend all the ingredients in a blender. You can add half a cup of strawberries, kiwi fruit or mango and a dash of grenadine for a particularly delicious drink.

Serves one

# French '75

**60 ml (2 fl oz) gin**
**30 ml (1 fl oz) lemon juice**
**15 ml ($^{1}/_{2}$ fl oz) sugar syrup**
**1 cup ice cubes**
**sparkling white wine or Champagne**
**long strips of lemon zest**

Pour the gin, lemon juice and sugar syrup into
a cocktail shaker over the ice cubes. Shake,
then pour into two Champagne flutes and top
up with the sparkling wine.

Garnish with the lemon zest.

Serves two

5

ga

# Gauguin

**1 lime**
**60 ml (2 fl oz) white rum**
**45 ml (1$^{1}/_{2}$ fl oz) golden rum**
**30 ml (1 fl oz) pineapple juice**
**1 cup ice cubes**
**crushed ice**
**cranberry juice to taste**

Juice the lime. Pour both types of rum and the pineapple and lime juices into a cocktail shaker over the ice cubes. Shake, then pour into two glasses filled with crushed ice. Top up with the cranberry juice.

Serves two

# Gimplet

**60 ml (2 fl oz) gin**
**30 ml (1 fl oz) lime cordial**
**30 ml (1 fl oz) fresh lime juice**
**1 cup ice cubes**
**lime wedge**

Pour the gin, cordial and lime juice into a
cocktail shaker over the ice cubes. Shake
sharply, then pour into a frosted Martini glass.
Garnish with a lime wedge.

Serves one

*You can make a traditional Gimlet by omitting
the lime juice, or a hard-to-pronounce
Gimblet, by omitting the lime cordial.*

gim

plet

# Harvey Wallbanger

**ice cubes**
**60 ml (2 fl oz) vodka**
**250 ml (8 fl oz) fresh orange juice**
**15 ml (¹/₂ fl oz) Galliano**

Place the ice cubes in a long glass. Pour the vodka over the ice and top up with the orange juice. Carefully pour in the Galliano.

Serves one

harvey
wallb

anger

# High Flyer

**ice cubes**
**30 ml (1 fl oz) Pernod**
**75 ml (2½ fl oz) fresh orange juice**
**splash of lemonade**

Place the ice cubes in a long glass. Pour the
Pernod over the ice and top up with the
orange juice. Finish with a splash of lemonade.

Serves one

# Japanese Slipper

**30 ml (1 fl oz) Midori**
**30 ml (1 fl oz) Cointreau**
**30 ml (1 fl oz) lemon juice**
**1 cup ice cubes**

Pour the Midori, Cointreau and lemon juice into
a cocktail shaker over the ice cubes. Shake,
then pour into a frosted Martini glass.

Serves one

# Long Tall Cowboy

**60 ml (2 fl oz) butterscotch schnapps**
**30 ml (1 fl oz) Bailey's Irish Cream**
**90 ml (3 fl oz) ice cold milk**
**1 cup ice cubes**

Pour the schnapps, Bailey's and milk into a cocktail shaker over the ice cubes. Shake, then strain into a long frosted glass.

Serves one

*This cowboy is an extended version of the delicious shooter, the C\*\*\* S\*\*\*\*\*\*\* Cowboy!*

long tall
co

maiden's

p

# Maiden's Prayer

**30 ml (1 fl oz) gin**
**30 ml (1 fl oz) white or golden rum**
**30 ml (1 fl oz) Cointreau**
**30 ml (1 fl oz) lemon juice**
**1 cup crushed ice**

Combine all the ingredients in a chilled cocktail shaker, shake and then strain into a frosted glass.

Serves one

*The Maiden's Prayer is called Between the Sheets when the gin is replaced with brandy or you've had one too many.*

# Margarita

**15 ml ($^1/_2$fl oz) lime juice**
**salt**
**1 cup ice cubes**
**20 ml ($^3/_4$ fl oz) lemon juice**
**30 ml (1 fl oz) tequila**
**40 ml (1$^1/_2$ oz) Cointreau**

Moisten the rim of a Margarita glass or an extra large
Martini glass with lime juice and dip it in salt. Put the ice
cubes into a cocktail shaker and add the lemon juice,
tequila and Cointreau. Shake, then strain into the glass.

You can make a Frozen Margarita by blending the ice,
lemon juice, tequila and Cointreau in a blender until
smooth and icy.

Serves one

*A Frozen Green Cactus Margarita can be made by*
*substituting Midori for the Cointreau.*

marg

arita

mar

# Martini

**50 ml (1$^3$/$_4$ oz) gin**
**whiff of dry vermouth**
**1 cup crushed ice**
**stuffed olive**

Pour the gin and vermouth into a cocktail shaker over
the crushed ice. Stir until well chilled, then strain and
pour into a frosted Martini glass.

Serves one

*There are endless versions of the Martini. A*
*traditional Martini is garnished with a stuffed olive.*
*If you substitute a cocktail onion for the olive, it is*
*called a Gibson. By substituting the gin with vodka*
*and garnishing with a lime wedge you create a*
*Diamond Martini. Swap the lime with a twist of*
*lemon and you have a Vodka Martini.*

# Emerald Martini

**50 ml (1³/₄ oz) gin**
**whiff of dry vermouth**
**1 cup crushed ice**
**dash of Midori**
**fresh red currants**

Pour the gin and vermouth into a cocktail shaker
over the crushed ice. Stir until well chilled, then
strain and pour into a frosted Martini glass with
the Midori. Garnish with the currants.

Serves one

ald
rtini

sapp

# Sapphire Martini

**50 ml (1³/₄ fl oz) Bombay Sapphire gin**
**whiff of dry vermouth**
**1 cup crushed ice**
**dash of blue curaçao or parfait d'amour**
**stuffed olive**

Pour the gin and vermouth into a cocktail shaker over the crushed ice. Stir until well chilled, then strain and pour into a frosted Martini glass with a dash of blue curaçao and the olive.

Serves one

hire
martini

# Mint Julep

**5 sprigs of mint**
**2 sugar cubes**
**crushed ice**
**50 ml (1³/₄ fl oz) bourbon**
**splash of soda or lemonade (optional)**

Crush the mint and the sugar cubes in the
bottom of a glass. Fill the glass with crushed ice,
then add the bourbon and stir.
Garnish with extra mint and add a splash of soda
or lemonade if desired.

Serves one

julep

# Mojito

**5 sprigs of mint**
**crushed ice**
**60 ml (2 fl oz) white or golden rum**
**1 teaspoon sugar syrup**
**dash of lime juice**
**soda water to taste**

Place the mint into a long glass with the crushed ice. Add the rum, sugar syrup and lime juice, then muddle (crush the mint with the back of a spoon and stir until the aroma of the mint is released). Keep stirring until chilled. Top up with soda water and stir again.

Serves one

*You can double the ingredients of this drink and serve it in a jug over ice.*

neg

# Negroni

**30 ml (1 fl oz) Campari**
**30 ml (1 fl oz) sweet vermouth**
**30 ml (1 fl oz) gin**
**ice cubes**
**strip of orange zest**

Place all the ingredients into a tumbler filled with the ice cubes. Stir and garnish with the orange zest.

Serves one

roni

# Old Fashioned

**1 sugar cube**
**2 dashes Angostura bitters**
**½ cup ice cubes**
**50 ml (1¾ fl oz) bourbon**
**strip of orange zest**

Saturate the sugar cube with bitters, then place into a tumbler with two ice cubes. Slowly pour in the bourbon, stirring with a bar spoon until the sugar is dissolved. Add more ice. Rub the orange zest around the rim of the glass before dropping the zest into the drink.

Serves one

*Sometimes the Old Fashioned is garnished with a maraschino cherry instead of orange zest.*

old fashioned

p

# Pegu

**65 ml (1$\frac{1}{2}$ fl oz) gin**
**15 ml ($\frac{1}{2}$ fl oz) Cointreau**
**15 ml ($\frac{1}{2}$ fl oz) lime juice**
**2 dashes Angostura bitters**
**ice cubes**
**twist of lime**

Place all the ingredients in a cocktail shaker over the ice and stir. Strain into a frosted Martini glass.

Garnish with the twist of lime if desired.

Serves one

# Pink Poodle

**grenadine**
**sugar**
**45 ml (1¹/₂ fl oz) vodka**
**90 ml (3 fl oz) pink grapefruit juice**
**1 cup ice cubes**

Run grenadine around the rim of a long glass
then dip it in sugar. Place the vodka and
grapefruit juice in a cocktail shaker over the
ice. Shake, then strain into the glass.

Serves one

*A Pink Poodle is a variation of the
Salty Dog, which is made with ordinary
grapefruit juice.*

pink

oodle

planter's p

# punch

## Planter's Punch

**50 ml (1³/₄ fl oz) golden rum**
**20 ml (³/₄ fl oz) lemon juice**
**60 ml (2 fl oz) fresh orange juice**
**dash of sugar syrup**
**2 cups ice cubes**
**soda water to taste**
**orange slice**

Place the first four ingredients in a cocktail shaker with half the ice cubes. Strain into a long glass filled with the remaining ice. Top up with soda water and garnish with an orange slice.

Serves one

# sangri

## Sangria

**1 x 750 ml (24 fl oz) bottle red wine**
**60 ml (2 fl oz) orange juice**
**60 ml (2 fl oz) lemon juice**
**4 teaspoons sugar syrup**
**2 cups ice cubes**

Combine all the ingredients in a large
jug and stir well. Serve in long glasses
garnished with citrus fruit.

You can make a peach Sangria by
substituting the sugar syrup with peach
schnapps. Garnish with slices of fresh
peach and red currants.

Serves eight

a

S

# Sea breeze

**1 cup ice cubes**
**60 ml (2 fl oz) vodka**
**dash of cranberry juice**
**dash of freshly squeezed grapefruit juice**
**cranberries**

Fill a long glass with the ice cubes and top with the remaining ingredients. Serve garnished with the cranberries.

Serves one

*You can make a Sea Change by adding a dash of fresh pineapple juice and substituting the grapefruit juice with freshly squeezed orange juice.*

ea
breeze

# Side Car

**45 ml (1¹/₂ fl oz) cognac or brandy**
**20 ml (³/₄ fl oz) Cointreau**
**20 ml (³/₄ fl oz) lemon juice**
**1 cup ice cubes**

Pour all of the ingredients into a cocktail shaker and shake sharply. Strain into a frosted Martini glass and garnish with a slice of orange or lemon.

Serves one

***For extra effect moisten the rim of the Martini glass with lemon and dip it in sugar.***

r

# Zombie

**90 ml (3 fl oz) rum**
**30 ml (1 fl oz) pineapple juice**
**30 ml (1 fl oz) lime juice**
**2 teaspoons sugar syrup**
**2 cups crushed ice**

Pour all the ingredients into a cocktail shaker,
shake and then strain into a tumbler or long glass.
For a stronger drink reduce the amount of ice.

Serves one

*A Zombie can be made with a combination of*
*white, golden and dark rum, so pick your*
*favourite blend. You can also add a dash of*
*papaya or mango juice to enhance the flavour.*
*Why not try making a sugar rim using coloured*
*jelly crystals?*

# index